RUSSIA

Keith Lye

Watts Books

London • New York • Sydney

Copyright © 1996

Original Edition 1987

Published in Great Britain by
Watts Books
96 Leonard Street
London EC2A 4RH

Published in Australia by
Franklin Watts Australia
14 Mars Road
Lane Cove
NSW 2006

ISBN: 0 7496 2022 6

Editor: Belinda Weber
Design: Val Carless
Illustrations: Gary Cookson
                Hayward Art Group

Photographs: Novosti 6B, 6T, 7T 8T, 9TL,
9TR, 9CL, 9CR, 9LR, 11B, 12T, 1±3T, 16B,
17TL, 17TR, 18T, 19T, 20T, 22T, 24T, 24B,
25TL, 25B, 28, 29TL, 29TR, 29C, 29B, 30T,
30B, 31T, 31B, 32T, 32B, 33T, 33C, 33B, 34T,
34BL, 34BR, 38T, 38BR, 39B, 40B, 41B, 43B,
44T, 44B, 45TL; Chris Fairclough: 20B, 25TR;
Hutchison Picture Library: 5T, 9B, 13B, Q9B,
35T; Stephen Keeler: 17B, 21B, 45TR; Kobal
Collection: 41TR; Popperfoto: 42BL, 42R, 45B;
John Massey Stewart: 7B, 22B, 23B, 42T,
43TL, 43TR; Zefa: 5B, 8B, 10T, 10B, 11TL,
11TR, 16T, 18B, 21T, 23T, 35B, 38BL, 39T, 40T,
41TL.

Printed in Belgium.

Contents

Introduction

Russia, which is also officially called the Russian Federation, is the world's largest country. It covers about a ninth of the world's land area and is nearly twice the size of Canada, the second largest country. Russia extends across two continents. About 25 per cent of its land area is in Europe and the rest is in Asia.

From 1922, Russia was part of the Union of Soviet Socialist Republics (USSR). The USSR, or Soviet Union, was a Communist country, made up of 15 republics. In 1991, following the failure of Soviet economic policies, the country's 15 republics split to become separate countries, the largest of which is Russia.

Twelve of these republics, excluding the three Baltic states of Estonia, Latvia and Lithuania, keep in contact through an organization called the Commonwealth of Independent States (CIS). Since 1991, Russia has faced many problems in reforming its economy and building a free enterprise system.

Above: These houses on the shores of Lake Baikal are built to withstand the cold. They are typical of those in the more remote Russian regions.

Below: Old churches, factories, modern offices and apartments can all be seen in this view of Moscow, Russia's capital and largest city.

The land

Russia stretches from the Baltic Sea in the west to the Pacific Ocean in the east. The maximum distance between east and west is about 9,700 km (6,000 miles). Russia includes eight time zones. At breakfast time in Vladivostok, in the far east, it is already late afternoon in Moscow. From north to south, Russia extends from the icy Arctic Ocean to the warm shores of the Black and Caspian seas. The greatest distance between north and south is 4,500 km (2,800 miles).

Most of Russia has long, cold, snowy winters and warm or hot summers. At Verkhoyansk, in the north-east, temperatures vary between -68°C (-90°F) in winter and 37°C (98°F) in summer. The warmest regions are in the south-west, between the Caspian and Black seas.

The precipitation (rain, snow, sleet and other forms of moisture) is generally light. Parts of the south-west and north-east have dry climates, with an average of less than 20 cm (8 inches) per year. The European plains in the west and the mountain regions throughout Russia have the greatest precipitation.

Above: No trees grow on the tundra, only small shrubs, grasses and lichens. Even in summer the ground just below the topsoil is frozen solid.

Below: A view of the bleak countryside of Sakhalin Island in eastern Siberia. The mountains are surrounded by taiga, forests of coniferous trees.

The far north is a frozen, treeless plain bordering the Arctic Ocean. This is the tundra. In summer, the top few centimetres of soil thaw, but below that lies the permafrost, ground that never thaws. South of the tundra lies the world's largest forest – the taiga. Conifers, such as Siberian larches, are the main trees in the taiga. South of the forests are grasslands, called steppes. Semi-desert and mountains lie in the far south.

Most of European Russia is flat or gently rolling country. In the south lie the Caucasus Mountains, containing Russia's highest point, Mount Elbrus. Asian Russia, east of the low Ural Mountains, is called Siberia. It is a vast region of plains, plateaux and mountains, with active volcanoes in the Kamchatka peninsula. Russia contains the world's deepest lake, Baikal, and part of the the world's largest lake, the Caspian Sea. Major rivers include the Lena in Asia and the Volga in Europe.

Above: A view of the Yenisey River as it flows through Krasnoyarsk in Siberia.

Below: Russian cowboys moving cattle through the grasslands of steppe country.

The people

About 82 per cent of the people in Russia are of Russian ancestry. They are the descendants of a group of people called the Slavs who lived in eastern Europe thousands of years ago. Historians divide the Slavs into three main groups: the East Slavs, the West Slavs and the South Slavs. The Russians are descended from the East Slavs. These people founded the first Russian state, called Kievan Rus, in the ninth century. After the Mongols defeated Kievan Rus in the 13th century, Moscow became the centre of Russian power.

Russian is the official language. It is written in the Cyrillic alphabet. This alphabet has letters that are written and pronounced differently from those of the Roman alphabet.

Russia has about 100 other ethnic groups. Minority groups include Tatars, Ukrainians, Chuvashes, Bashkirs, Belarussians, Mordovians, Chechens, Germans, Udmurts, Mari, Kazakhs, Avars, Armenians and Jews. Small groups of Aleuts, Chukchi, Inuit (Eskimo) and Koryaks live in the far north of Siberia.

Above: An old woman and a child from Sakhalin Island. Their features show that they are descendants of original Mongol inhabitants.

Below: A general view of the river flowing through St Petersburg. In the foreground one of its large parks can be seen.

Above: Schoolchildren aged between 7-8 learn about computers.

Below: A construction worker from Buryat Autonomous Republic.

Above: Andrei Bogachev is a traffic policeman in Moscow.

Below: Weaver Valentina Golubeva training workers at Ivanovo.

Many of Russia's minority groups have their own language. But many individuals also speak Russian as their second language. Because of its mixed population, Russia is a federation consisting of 21 republics, six territories, 49 provinces, 10 autonomous (self-governing) areas, two cities with federal status (Moscow and St Petersburg) and the autonomous Jewish region of Birobijan in the far south-east. In the early 1990s, some minority peoples have asked for a greater degree of self-rule. For example, the Chechens declared their area, the Chechen Republic, independent in 1991. But Russia did not recognize this act.

Religious worship was discouraged when Russia was under Communist rule. But, from the late 1980s, the government allowed religious groups to organize. Church attendance grew quickly. The chief religious group is the Russian Orthodox Church. Other groups include Roman Catholics, Protestants, Muslims and Jews.

Above: An outdoor bookstall in Nizhny-Novgorod.

Below: Children in traditional uniform at an elementary school.

Where people live

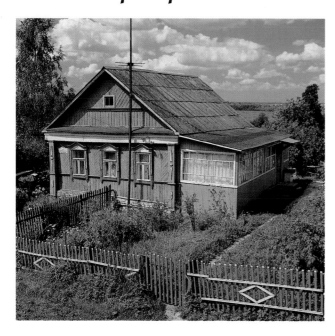

Above: A typical wooden peasant cottage with a green picket fence in Moscow.

Below: Flats in Moscow. Migration from the countryside to the cities has caused overcrowding.

In 1993, Russia had a population of about 148 million. Only China, India, the United States, Indonesia and Brazil have larger populations. Almost 80 per cent of the people live in European Russia which has a population density of about 28 per square kilometre (72 per square mile). By contrast, Siberia has an average population density of only 2 people per square kilometre (6 per square mile).

Increased mechanization and efficiency in agriculture has meant that fewer farm workers are needed than in the past and so many young people have moved into urban areas, where living conditions and leisure facilities are usually better. As a result, Russia has become an urbanized country, with 74 per cent of the people in the cities and towns. Moscow and St Petersburg are the largest cities. Russia also has 11 other cities with populations of more than one million and more than 30 with populations of over 500,000.

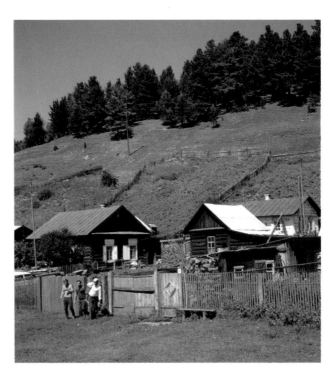

Left: The old section of town, Ulyanovsk.

Above: Houses at Listvyanka, a village near Irkutsk on the shores of Lake Baikal.

Below: A motorized sledge roars over the snow in the Kamchatka Peninsula of eastern Siberia. Such sledges have made life easier in the harsh climate.

Migration from the countryside to the cities, especially Moscow, the most popular destination, has produced labour shortages in some remote areas. During the Communist period, the government offered special facilities to attract people to eastern Siberia and live in new settlements to develop the area's rich natural resources. Meanwhile, the cities became overcrowded. The situation became worse during World War II (1939-1945), when over a million houses and apartment buildings were destroyed.

Housing shortages continue to this day. For example, about a fifth of city dwellers have to share their homes with another family. Most urban people live in rented apartments or small houses. Few own their homes, and young married couples have to wait for several years before getting their own apartment. However, private ownership has been encouraged since the break-up of the former Soviet Union.

In rural areas, many families have their own houses, though some remote areas lack such facilities as electricity, gas and running water.

Moscow

Moscow became the national capital of what was to become the Soviet Union in 1918. But the origins of the city go back about 800 years, when settlers on the north bank of the Moskva River, where Moscow stands today, built a kreml, a walled fortress. Inside the walls were the most important buildings, such as churches, a palace and arsenals. Several Russian cities began as kremlins (the English form of kreml).

The Moscow Kremlin is the seat of Russia's national government. In it are magnificent domed churches and cathedrals, a former royal palace, museums and government offices. The Kremlin Palace of Congresses, built in 1961, was the meeting place of the Soviet Communist party from 1961 to 1990.

Moscow is a city of theatres, concert halls, cinemas, museums and libraries. Muscovites think of themselves as the most cultured people in Russia, though the people of Russia's former capital of St Petersburg (called Leningrad in Communist times) challenge this claim.

Above: St Basil's Cathedral, Red Square, in the heart of Moscow, is made up on nine chapels each with its own elaborately decorated roof.

Below: Some of the landmarks of Moscow. They show the contrast between the old part of the city and the new capital.

1. Zoo	4. Museum	7. St. Basil's Cathedral	10. Fine Arts Museum
2. Planetarium	5. Red Square	8. The Kremlin	11. Swimming Pool
3. Bolshoi Theatre	6. Gum	9. Library	12. Sports Stadium

North-east of the Kremlin is Red Square, where the former Communist government held huge parades on special occasions. Landmarks in Red Square include St Basil's Cathedral and, beneath the Kremlin's eastern wall, a mausoleum where visitors could see the embalmed body of Vladimir Lenin, leader of the Communist Russian Revolution in 1917.

The Moscow Metro is the most elegant underground rail line in the world. Its 141 stations, decorated with marble, granite and crystal, are kept spotless by armies of cleaners. It carries about 7,000,000 passengers a day along its 227 km (141 miles) of track.

Muscovites eat 170 tonnes of ice cream every day, even when winter temperatures drop to –10°C (14°F). They are also animal lovers who keep thousands of cats, dogs and birds. Like other Soviet city dwellers, they like to spend much of their leisure time in the surrounding countryside. Some are lucky enough to own a dacha, a country cottage.

Above: Arbat, in the older part of Moscow, was the first street in the city for pedestrians only. In fair weather it is full of people shopping.

Below: Even in late spring snow, Moscow citizens like to drink their coffee or chocolate at an open-air cafe.

Fact file: land and population

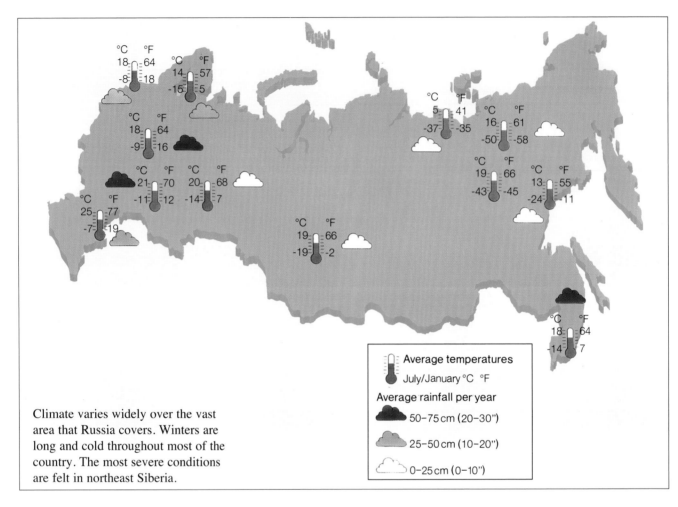

Climate varies widely over the vast area that Russia covers. Winters are long and cold throughout most of the country. The most severe conditions are felt in northeast Siberia.

Average temperatures
July/January °C °F

Average rainfall per year
50–75 cm (20–30")
25–50 cm (10–20")
0–25 cm (0–10")

▷ **Land area comparison**
With an area of 17,005,000 sq km (6,592,800 sq miles), Russia is nearly twice as big as the United States and 70 times larger than the United Kingdom.

RUSSIA   **USA**   **AUSTRALIA**   **UK**

Key Facts

Location: Russia is the world's largest country. It straddles Europe and Asia. The mainland extends roughly between latitudes 41° and nearly 78° North, and between longitudes 28° East and 170° West.
Area: 17,075,000 sq km (6,592,800 sq miles)
Population: 148,000,000 (1993)
Capital: Moscow

Major cities
(with populations):
Moscow (8,747,000)
St. Petersburg
   (formerly Leningrad, 4,437,000)
Novosibirsk (1,442,000)
Nizhny Novgorod
   (formerly Gorki, 1,441,000)
Yekaterinburg
   (formerly Sverdlovsk, 1,371,000)

Highest point: Mount Elbrus in the Caucasus Mountains, 5,642 m (18,520 ft) above sea level
Longest river: (entirely within Russia): Lena, 4,400 km (2,734 miles); (longest in the European part of Russia): Volga, 3,531 km (2,194 miles).
Largest lake: Caspian Sea, which has a total area of 370,370 sq km (143,000 sq miles).

Russia 9 per sq km

USA 27 per sq km

Australia 2 per sq km

Britain 234 per sq km

Japan 333 per sq km

France 105 per sq km

▽ **Where people live**
Nearly three times as many people live
in cities and towns as in rural areas.

◁ **A population density comparison**
In world terms, Russia's population
density is extremely low. This is because
so much of Asian Russia (Siberia) is
almost empty of people.

St. Petersburg

Moscow

Nizhny Novgorod

Samara

Yekaterinburg

Novosibirsk

△ **Major population centres**
Most of Russia's largest cities are
situated in the western (European) part
of the country, where the main industrial
areas are found.

🏢 Major cities
〰 Main routeways

Home life

In 1991, the birth rate in Russia was estimated to be 12 per 1,000 people, which is less than half of the world average figure. One reason for the low birth rate is the shortage of good housing in the inner cities.

The housing shortage was also one of the causes of the social discontent that led to the introduction of reforms in the Soviet Union in the 1980s. For example, in 1987, an estimated 17 per cent of Soviet citizens did not have their own dwelling. Many newly married couples have to live with their parents for several years before they can find a home of their own. In 1987, experts estimated that a couple wanting state housing had to wait 10 to 15 years before they were accommodated.

The average family apartment in Russia has two rooms, used for both living and sleeping. The apartment also contains a small, eat-in kitchen, a bathroom, a toilet, a small entrance hall and perhaps a balcony.

Above: A Russian family dining in a typical town apartment in Satka, south of the Ural Mountains.

Right: Weddings are a time for celebration. This happy wedding party with three married couples is crossing Red Square in the heart of Moscow.

Under Communist rule, the production of consumer goods had a lower priority than heavy industry. As a result, many household items, common in Western homes, were often difficult to obtain in the Soviet Union. Since the reforms of the 1980s and the break-up of the Soviet Union in 1991, standards of living have improved, especially for people in the bottom 10 per cent of the population. But some popular domestic items, such as video recorders, remain in short supply.

More than 90 per cent of Russian families now have a refrigerator and 80 per cent have a washing machine. Almost all families have a television set, though many are still in black and white. Nearly one fifth of households owns a car and nearly 70 per cent have a bicycle.

Health care remains free, though private health-care services are developing. Officially, unemployment is low, but this is partly the result of government aid to industries that may eventually disappear as competition increases in the new Russia, with its increasingly free-enterprise economy.

Above left: Celebrating a birthday, Russian style. Here a grandmother poses for a photograph surrounded by her children and grandchildren.

Above: A five-year-old's birthday party in her family's Moscow apartment.

Below: Cats are popular family pets among people who live in cities.

Shops and shopping

Shopping in Russian cities and towns can be an exhausting business. Until recently all shops used the 'three-line' system. Under it, customers line up to order the goods they want to buy. The shop assistant removes the goods from the shelf or display case, writes the order on a ticket and hands it to the customer. The customer then waits at the cash desk to pay for the goods. The cashier takes the money and stamps the ticket. The customer returns to the sales counter for another long wait to give the stamped ticket to the assistant, who hands over the goods, usually wrapped in paper and tied with string.

This tedious and time-consuming system is still used in many toyshops, bookshops and some clothes shops and food shops. It has been replaced in the large department stores and new food supermarkets in some of the larger cities by the Western system of paying at the counter or check-out. From the 1980s, shops have been better stocked, but long lines of people waiting to buy what they need are still common sights throughout Russia.

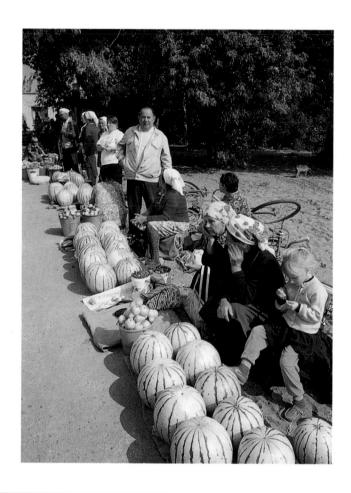

Above: Farmers selling their produce by the side of the road. This is popular in small villages and rural areas.

Left: A McDonalds restaurant in Moscow. Familiar Western fast-food restaurants are becoming more popular in Russia's larger cities.

Left: Inside Cheryomushki supermarket in Moscow. In such supermarkets the Western system of paying at check-out desks has been introduced, which cuts down on shopping time.

Below: GUM is Moscow's largest department store. It stands on Red Square, opposite the Kremlin. GUM stands for Gosudartsvenniy Universalniy Magazin (State Department Store).

Russia still has difficulty in distributing food and consumer products so that they reach everyone. Efficient distribution and rising prices are two major problems faced by Russian shoppers in the 1990s.

Retired grandmothers are useful for shopping. While the rest of the family is at school or at work these older members can search the shops and markets for newly delivered foodstuffs.

Although such searching is becoming less necessary as food distribution improves, few women – who do most of the shopping – go out without carrying a bag so that they can take advantage of unexpected supplies in the stores.

One of the less desirable developments arising from Russia's gradual change from a Communist to a free enterprise economy has been the growth of a 'black economy'. This enables citizens to buy almost anything they want, if they can afford the black market prices.

Cooking and eating

The food eaten by Russian citizens is traditional. It reflects their various ethnic origins – although pizza and hamburger bars are now appearing in Moscow.

Breakfast is a quick, light meal. It may consist of slices of rye bread, a piece of cheese and tea. Dinner, the main meal of the day, includes a meat dish with potatoes and other vegetables. This may be followed by a simple dessert of fresh fruit or cake. Russians are fond of meat, so supper will probably include another meat dish, after a bowl of shchi (a cabbage soup). People eat large quantities of bread and usually drink sweet black tea with most meals.

No Russian table is complete without its samovar, an urn in which water is boiled to make tea. The teapot itself usually sits on top of the samovar to keep hot.

Above: A selection of the kind of foods that Russian people like to eat. They include fresh salads, roast pork and a mug of rich soup.

Right: A typical family meal in Russia. The ornate samovar (tea urn) dominating the table is a very common sight in Russian homes. People throughout Russia drink sweet black tea.

Left: A traditional Kasha festival near Zainsk. Kasha is a dish made from crushed or powdered buckwheat. It is usually baked in the oven, then mixed with butter.

Below: A poster warning against alcoholism. Russian citizens used to drink more hard liquor than people in many other countries.

Traditional Russian dishes include borscht, a pungent soup made with chopped beetroot, onions, tomatoes, shredded cabbage and diced sausages. Meat stock, herbs and slivers of mutton or beef are added, and the borscht is served with sour cream. It may be followed by hot pirozhki (meat pasties) and sweet bliny (pancakes with jam and sour cream).

Traditionally meals were washed down with iced vodka. Until recently, Soviet citizens drank more alcoholic spirits than any other people – an average of 14 litres (25 pints) a year for every person aged over 15. In 1985 the price of vodka quadrupled as part of the government's intensive anti-drinking campaign. The campaign has been successful in the towns, but less so in the countryside where illegal vodka is distilled.

In the early 1990s, rising prices caused by inflation and economic reforms led to changes in Russian eating habits. Bread and egg consumption increased at the expense of meat and fruits. Also, people tend to be less hospitable than in the past, when inviting friends and relatives to meals was an important part of social life.

Pastimes and sports

Chess is the most popular pastime in Russia, and millions of people learn to play the game to a high standard at an early age. In summer, open-air chess games in parks or on quiet street corners are a common sight. They attract large crowds of spectators, young and old, who follow each move with fascination. The country has produced many grandmasters and about a dozen world champions, among them Gary Kasparov and Anatoly Karpov.

Another popular pastime is stamp collecting and there are thousands of stamp clubs.

Millions of people in Russia enjoy regular visits to the cinema. In the 1980s, the Soviet Union produced about 180 feature films a year. In 1991, the number soared to 400. But then production shrank as a result of the proposed break-up of government-supported film organizations. Russia has many museums which are popular attractions with families. Some, like the Hermitage Museum in St Petersburg, attract visitors from all over the world.

Above: In warm weather people flock to lakeside and seaside resorts around the Black Sea to swim. Some people even bathe in the ice-covered rivers.

Below: Soccer is popular throughout Russia, from local teams that play in parks to the country's successful international teams.

Left: Lakes in Siberia freeze solid in winter and are safe for children to play on. Here a group of children are skating, sleighing and trying to play ice-hockey.

Below: Spectators take a keen interest as people play chess at Gorki Park, Moscow.

More than half the people take an annual holiday away. Moscow and the sunny Black Sea resorts are the favourite places. Travel is relatively cheap. Travel companies belong to the state or such organizations as trade unions.

Organized sports play an important part in the daily life of most Russian citizens. There are thousands of physical training clubs, sports halls, swimming pools and stadiums, all of which are open free to all citizens. Schools also encourage physical education. It is hardly surprising that Russians win so many medals for sport and gymnastics in international competitions. Soccer is the leading sport. Track and field events, volleyball, skiing and basket-ball are all popular, while ice hockey, skating and skiing attract many people in winter.

Russia's ethnic minorities also have their own traditional forms of exercise. The Yakuts of central Siberia are skilled reindeer-sled racers. Archery is popular with the Buryats of eastern Siberia. On the Amur River in south-eastern Russia, canoeing is a popular sport.

News and broadcasting

Before 1917 more than 75 per cent of the Russian people were illiterate. Today, almost everyone can read. People spend, on average, almost one-sixth of their free time doing so. To meet this demand, Russia has become a major producer of newspapers, magazines and books. Under Communist rule, the government expected the press to play a major role in the political and moral education of the people. This meant the media were heavily censored.

In 1991, a press law encouraged the growth of the publishing industry. The readership of radical publications soared, while the number of subscribers to official Communist newspapers fell dramatically. By 1992, Russia had more than 4,800 officially registered newspapers and nearly 9,700 periodicals. Leading dailies were Izvestiya, Komosomolskaya Pravda, and Trud. In 1993, President Boris Yeltsin announced the banning of several newspapers and the dismissals of the editors of Pravda, the old Communist party paper, and Sovetskaya Rossiya, which expressed extreme nationalist views.

Above: Vladimir Nazarov, a Russian radio reporter, interviews workers on the 24th floor of a new apartment building which is under construction.

Below: Presenters Aza Likhitchenko and Igor Kirilov in a Moscow television studio. Russian television emphasizes serious and educational programmes.

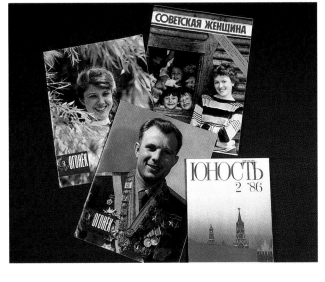

Above left: A selection of children's books, ranging from fairy tales to how-to-do-it books.

Above: Russian readers have lots of magazines to choose from, ranging from serious political reading to tabloids.

Below: Some of the newspapers published when Russia was part of the Soviet Union. The Soviet media expressed the government's views.

Soviet radio and television services were more serious than those in the West. They broadcast many news and documentary programmes, classical music, sport and cartoons for children. Violence was censored and most programmes were educational.

Since 1990, censorship has been relaxed and advertising is now permitted. Television and radio broadcasting comes under the Russian Federal Television and Radio Broadcasting Service, established in 1993. The two main channels are Ostankino and All-Russian State Television. There are also local city channels. About 98 per cent of Russians can receive TV broadcasts. Satellite TV reached five per cent of the people in 1993. Cable TV is also available in some areas. Access to Western influences increased in the 1990s. Russian teenagers enjoy popular music, especially from Britain and the United States. Russia even has some rock bands and discos are becoming more common.

Fact file: home and leisure

Key facts

Population composition: In 1992 people under 15 years of age made up 22.6 per cent of the population; people between 15 and 59 made up 60.9 per cent, and people over 60 made up 16.5 per cent. Women formed 53 per cent of the population.

Average life expectancy: 69 years in 1992. By comparison, people in the United States have an average life expectancy of 77 years, whereas people in India live, on average, 61 years. In 1992, Russian women had an average life expectancy of 75 years, 11 years longer than Russian men.

Rate of population increase: 0.5 per cent per year between 1985 and 1992, as compared with the world average of 1.7 per cent. On current trends, the population is expected to decline to about 143.5 million in the year 2010.

Family life: The marriage rate in 1991 was 8.6 per 1,000 people. The average number in a household was 3.2.

Homes: The average size of a town house or apartment is 14.1 sq m (152 sq ft). Rents, payable to the state, are low at about 12 per cent of net income.

Work: The total work force in 1991 was 73,800,000, or 89.6 per cent of people between 16 and 59. Women made up 52 per cent of this figure. The five-day week was introduced in 1967. The average working week is now 40 hours. The minimum wage in 1993 was 7,740 roubles per month.

Religions: The Soviet government discouraged religious worship and many young people are non-religious. But from the late 1980s, many churches and monasteries were re-opened and religious freedoms restored under a 'freedom of conscience' law. All religions are now equal before the law and the main church, the Russian Orthodox Church, has an estimated 35 to 40 million adherents. Other groups include Protestants, Roman Catholics, Muslims and Jews.

19%	69%	92%	92%	100%
Cars	**Bicycles**	**Central heating**	**Refrigerator**	**Television**

Alcoholic drinks 4%

Culture 6%

Furniture and household appliances 10%

Housing, taxes and financial payments 15%

Clothing and footwear 25%

Food 40%

△ **How many households owned goods in 1992**
Ownership of household and other consumer goods has increased rapidly in recent years. Most homes have television sets, refrigerators and central heating. But car ownership remains low by comparison with Western countries.

◁ **How the average household budget was spent in 1992**
Food accounts for a third of household spending in Russia. Expenditure on alcoholic drinks has declined in recent years because of a government campaign against alcohol abuse.

▽ **Soviet currency**
The unit of currency is the rouble, divided into 100 kopecks. In 1994, officially, £1 = 0.87 roubles (US $1 = 0.59 roubles), but the market rate was £1 = 2,520 roubles ($1 = 1,691 roubles).

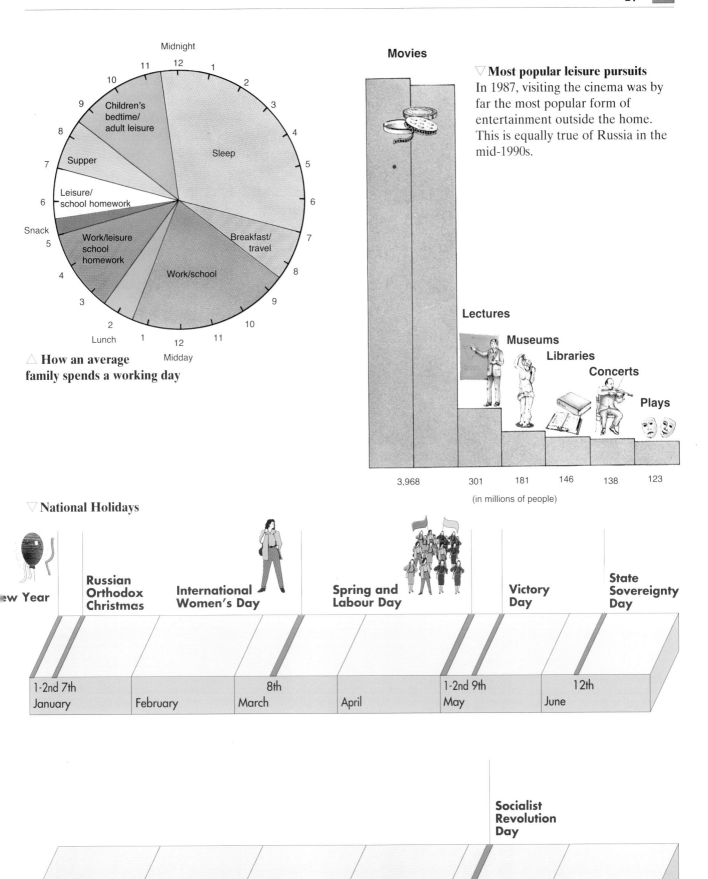

△ **How an average family spends a working day**

Midnight

Children's bedtime/adult leisure

Sleep

Supper

Leisure/school homework

Snack

Work/leisure school homework

Breakfast/travel

Work/school

Lunch

Midday

Movies

▽ **Most popular leisure pursuits**
In 1987, visiting the cinema was by far the most popular form of entertainment outside the home. This is equally true of Russia in the mid-1990s.

Lectures

Museums

Libraries

Concerts

Plays

3,968   301   181   146   138   123

(in millions of people)

▽ **National Holidays**

New Year | Russian Orthodox Christmas | International Women's Day | Spring and Labour Day | Victory Day | State Sovereignty Day

1-2nd 7th January | February | 8th March | April | 1-2nd 9th May | 12th June

Socialist Revolution Day

July | August | September | October | 7-8th November | December

Farming and fishing

Under Communism, the government owned all farmland and industries. Farmland was divided between state farms and collectives. State farms employed workers who were paid by the state. Collective farms were jointly owned by all who worked on them and wages were paid as equal shares out of the profits the farm made. Each worker had a private plot for private use. These private plots were often more productive than the land belonging to the collective.

When the Soviet Union broke up in 1991, private ownership of the land was permitted and state farms and collective were encouraged to register as co-operatives or share companies. By 1992, 77 per cent of the former farms had re-registered, though some preferred to remain as state or collective farms.

In 1993, a law permitted free sale of land and the borrowing of money to develop it. But, progress was slow in privatising land ownership though, in some areas, farm workers banded together to set up private farms.

Above: A worker with a fine crop of peppers that have been grown in glasshouses on a collective farm in the Stavropol region north of the Caucasus Mountains.

Right: Combine harvesters and other farm machinery are used on Russia's large wheat farms.

Russia has vast areas of fertile land, especially in the black earth region in the southern steppes. However, most of Russia has a short growing season. Droughts periodically affect 60 per cent of Russia's best farmland, while occasional storms do much damage. When crops fail, Russia has to import food, especially grains. Yet in normal years, Russia is one of the world's leading producers of barley, oats, rye and wheat.

Other major crops include flax, fruits, potatoes and other vegetables, sugar beet and sunflowers (for making sunflower oil). Cattle, sheep and pig farming has become increasingly important since the 1970s, while people in the northern tundra have herds of reindeer.

Fishing is important off the north coast and also in the Atlantic and Pacific oceans. Fishing vessels also operate in the Caspian Sea which contains sturgeon which yield the delicacy caviar. But, since the break-up of the Soviet Union in 1991, several nations now compete for this valuable product.

Above left: Fish experts examine sterlets, small sturgeon taken from the Amur River in eastern Siberia.

Below: A tea plantation in southern Kranoyarsk Region.

Above right: Harvesting grapes at Kuban in the southern part of the Krasnoyarsk Region of central Siberia.

Natural resources and industry

Before 1917, Russia was a backward country, whose economy depended mainly on agriculture. Under Communist rule, the Soviet Union became a leading industrial power. Russia has rich natural resources, including huge forests, abundant hydroelectric power, and many mineral deposits. Oil is extracted in several areas, including the Urals, the Sea of Azov, the Black Sea area and western Siberia. The country has abundant iron ore and coal, which are used to make steel. Russia also has rich reserves of copper, gold, lead, platinum, tin, lead, zinc and various rare metals. Mines in Siberia produce large quantities of diamonds.

Much of Russia's manufacturing industry is based in the west, in European Russia. Moscow and St Petersburg are leading manufacturing cities, while other industrial centres are situated along the Volga River and in the Ural Mountains region.

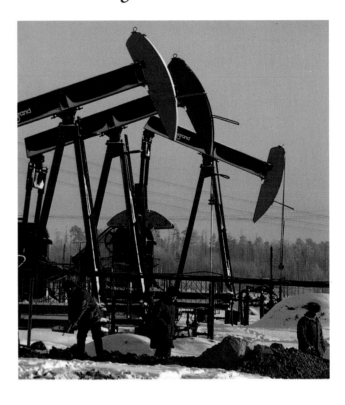

Above: Refining oil in Nizhnevartovsk. Russia has very rich natural resources and oil is extracted in many areas.

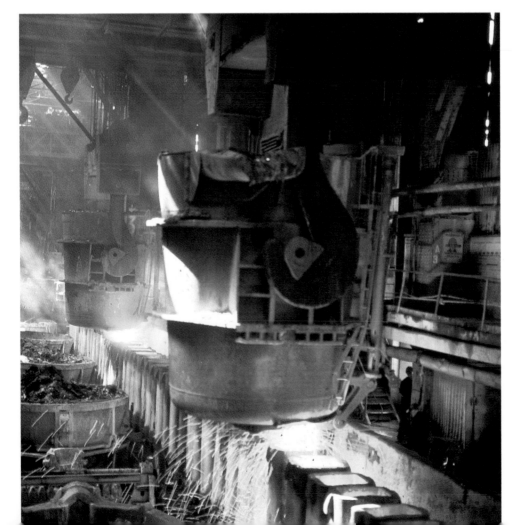

Left: Pouring molten steel at one of Russia's largest steel works at Magnitogorsk. This city is south-west of Chelyabinsk, in the southern Urals. It is a major industrial city.

Manufacturing is the most valuable activity in Russia. Under Communist rule, the government developed many state-owned industries, producing heavy machinery, tractors and electrical equipment, while St Petersburg builds ships and other equipment. Chemicals, chemical products and oil refining are also important. Processed food, paper and textiles are also produced.

After the break-up of the Soviet Union in 1991, Russia began to convert its government-controlled industries into a privately-owned ones. New businesses, some joint ventures with foreign companies, are being set up. Many new factories are making consumer goods, which were in short supply in the former Soviet Union. Russia has also obtained foreign technical assistance to modernize its older industries. This state of upheaval caused severe inflation, a fall in industrial production, and the collapse of some industries. Russia also faces another challenge – reducing the pollution caused by industry. Despite all these problems, Russia's great natural resources and skilled work force give hope for economic recovery.

Above: Open mining of coal at Kholboljinski mine in the Buryat Autonomous Republic, east of Lake Baikal. This region is rich in minerals, such as iron, titanium and tungsten.

Below: Gold, mined in Yakutia, which has two of the country's major goldfields. Russia is one of the world's leading producers of this rare and valuable metal.

Soviet technology

In the years following World War II (1939-1945), Soviet technology concentrated on rebuilding its heavy industries, which had been destroyed or badly damaged by warfare. In the 1950s, Soviet technologists began to work on developing aerospace industries. Several hundred spacecraft were launched every year. Most were artificial satellites intended for communications or meteorological purposes. There were also delivery supply flights carrying crews, food, water and even fresh air to the country's orbiting space research stations.

The Soviet Union launched the first artificial Earth satellite, Sputnik 1, in October 1957. A month later, Sputnik 2 carried a dog named Laika beyond the Earth's atmosphere. Two years later Luna 2 was the first space probe to land on the Moon. Soviet cosmonaut Yuri Gagarin (1934-1968) became the first human to orbit the Earth in his spacecraft Vostok 1 in 1961.

Above: The Soviet ice-breaker Lenin was the world's first non-naval nuclear-powered ship.

Right: A Soyuz spacecraft blasts off to carry three Soviet cosmonauts into space. Some Soyuz missions have lasted for more than two month and made a thousand orbits of the Earth.

The Soviet Union scored several other space firsts. They included the first woman in space, Valentina Tereshkova (Vostok 6, 1963); the first docking of two manned spacecraft and exchange of crews (Soyuz 4 and Soyuz 5, 1969); and the launch of the first experimental space station (Salyut 1, 1971). In 1987-1988, Colonel Vladimir Titov and Flight Engineer Musa Manarov achieved the longest manned space flight, lasting 365 days, 22.66 hours.

The break-up of the Soviet Union in 1991 appeared to threaten the country's space research. This was because Baykonur, the Soviet space centre from which all the manned flights were launched, was in Kazakhstan, north-east of the Aral Sea. But in 1994, Russia agreed to rent the space centre for 20 years.

Soviet scientists and technologists made many other important achievements. But, in seeking to keep up in the arms race with the West, the Soviet Union diverted more and more of its efforts into military spending. This weakened the Soviet economy and was a major factor in the final collapse of the Soviet Union.

Above left: A giant MI-6 helicopter airlifts a portable building across difficult country for workers on the Baikal-Amur Mainline.

Above right: Coloured lights trace out the movements of a cybernetic machine, or 'robot'.

Below: The Vilnisk power station is one of many hydroelectric projects being developed to meet the needs of Russian industry.

Transportation

The sheer size of Russia makes it essential to run an extensive and efficient system of transportation. For example, London is nearer to New York City across the Atlantic Ocean than Moscow in European Russia is to Vladivostok on the Pacific coast.

The Russian climate is unkind to roads. In the spring thaw, many road surfaces break up because of frost damage and become impassable seas of mud. Distances between major cities are long and the country still has no major west-east highway link. Almost twice as much freight is carried by rail as by truck.

A rail line across Siberia, built between 1891 and 1916, links Moscow and Vladivostok. It runs close to the frontiers with Mongolia and China. In 1984, a new stretch of line was completed, running to the Amur River and the Pacific coast. This line is intended to open up the frozen, mineral-rich region north of Lake Baikal. It is known as the Baikal-Amur Mainline, or the BAM for short.

Private cars are expensive in Russia. But public transport, including internal flights, is good and cheap.

Above: Workers put the finishing touches to a new Vaz 2108 car.

Below left: Building the Baikal-Amur Mainline. The permafrost is so unstable that in places the railbed had to settle for two years before trains could run over it.

Below: A modern high-speed express train waits at Volgograd station. More than half the rail network is electrified.

In parts of Russia, where the climate is less harsh, waterways are important in carrying goods and raw materials. The Volga, which flows into the Caspian Sea, is the main river used for transportation. Canals link it to the Baltic Sea, the River Don and the Black Sea and also to the Moskva River and Moscow. Ice-breaking ships work to keep northern rivers and seaports open in winter, but the most northerly ports become ice-bound and have to be closed between November and March.

The leading seaports include Archangelsk, Murmansk, Nakhodka, St Petersburg and Vladivostok. Another port, Kaliningrad, serves the small Russian enclave on the Baltic Sea between Poland and Lithuania. The Soviet airline Aeroflot was originally set up in 1923 and it became the largest airline of all time. But since 1990, the huge fleet has been operated by more than 40 domestic operators.

Above: A station on the Circle Line of the Moscow Metro. This is the most elegant underground system in the world.

Below: A sleigh drawn by reindeer races over the snow near Murmansk, the country's chief Arctic Ocean port.

Fact file: economy and trade

▽ **The distribution of Russian economic activity**
Most industries and farming areas are in western
Russia. Siberia is comparatively under-developed.

	Industry
	Petroleum
	Natural gas
	Iron ore
	Coal

	Gold
	Cereals
	Potatoes
	Sugar beet
	Cotton

	Cattle
	Sheep
	Reindeer
	Forest products
	Fishing

Key Facts

Structure of production: Of the total gross domestic product, farming, forestry and fishing contribute about 13 per cent; industry 49 per cent; and services 39 per cent.

Farming: About 7 per cent of the land in Russia is used for farming crops. Russia also has large areas of meadows and pastures for grazing. They make up about 5 per cent of Russia. Main products: barley, eggs, fruits, dairy products, meat, milk, oats, potatoes and other vegetables, rye, sugar beet, sunflower seeds, wheat, wool. Livestock: cattle, 20,600,000; sheep, 55,200,000; pigs, 35,400,000.

Forestry: Forests cover about 46 per cent of the land. Not surprisingly, Russia is one of the world's leading producers of coniferous wood.

Mining: Russia's rich natural resources include oil, natural gas and coal. It is also a major producer of copper, diamonds, gold, iron ore, platinum, lead, tin, zinc and rare metals.

Transportation: roads: 893,000 km (554,900 miles), 74 per cent paved, vehicles(1992) – passenger cars, 9,661,000, trucks and buses 465,000; rail: 158,100 km (98,241 miles); airports (1993): 58; shipping: the merchant marine carried 464 million tonnes of cargo (1991).

Trade (1991): Total imports: US $43,500 million; exports: US $58,700 million.

Public administration and defence 3.3%

Other 6%

Agriculture 13.5%

Finance and services 19.9%

Trade 7.6%

Transport and communications 7.8%

Construction 14.6%

Mining, manufacturing and public utilities 27.3%

◁**The distribution of the Russian labour force by industry in 1991** Industry and agriculture employ two-fifths of workers, but the service sector is expanding.

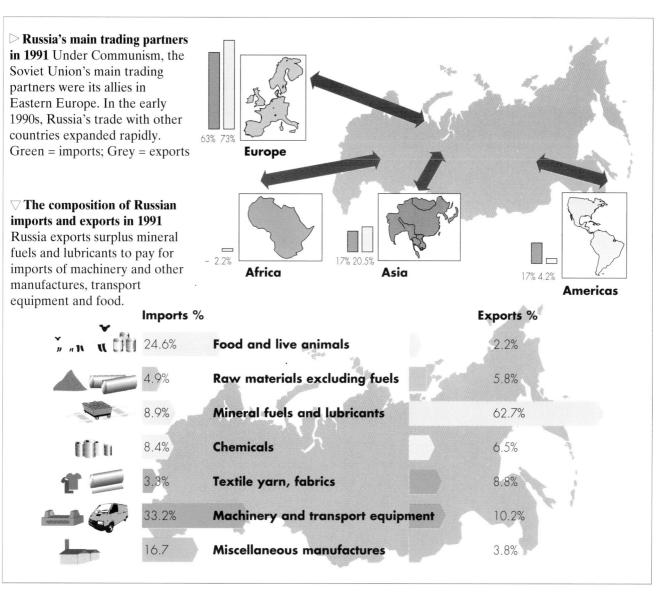

▷ **Russia's main trading partners in 1991** Under Communism, the Soviet Union's main trading partners were its allies in Eastern Europe. In the early 1990s, Russia's trade with other countries expanded rapidly. Green = imports; Grey = exports

63% 73%
Europe

– 2.2%
Africa

17% 20.5%
Asia

17% 4.2%
Americas

▽ **The composition of Russian imports and exports in 1991** Russia exports surplus mineral fuels and lubricants to pay for imports of machinery and other manufactures, transport equipment and food.

Imports %		Exports %
24.6%	**Food and live animals**	2.2%
4.9%	**Raw materials excluding fuels**	5.8%
8.9%	**Mineral fuels and lubricants**	62.7%
8.4%	**Chemicals**	6.5%
3.3%	**Textile yarn, fabrics**	8.8%
33.2%	**Machinery and transport equipment**	10.2%
16.7	**Miscellaneous manufactures**	3.8%

Education

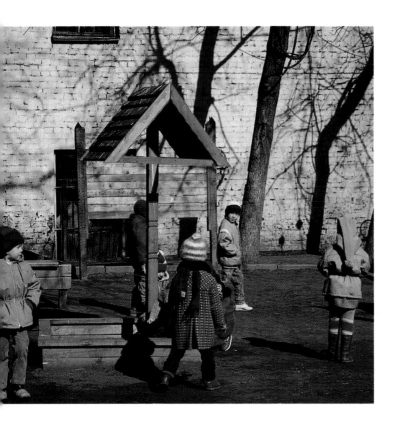

Free, compulsory education is available for all children between the ages of 7 and 17. Most children attend pre-school kindergarten and continue in further education after they are 17. Even remote areas have a full education service. Under Communist rule, all schools were run by the state. But in the 1990s, some private, fee-paying schools had opened. By 1992, Russia had about 200 non-state schools, with more than 20,000 pupils, while some institutions of higher education had begun to charge tuition fees.

Most children attend school six days a week. The school day begins at 8.30 a.m. and ends at 2.30 p.m. Pupils study basic subjects including Russian, which is compulsory, though ethnic minorities have the right to teaching and textbooks in their own languages. Other basic subjects include mathematics, geography, history, social studies and a foreign language. English is the most popular foreign language.

Above: A kindergarten playground in Moscow.

Below: Members of the Young Pioneers gather round a campfire at Bratsk, in Irkutsk.

Right: A Moscow secondary school student uses a computer during a mathematics lesson.

There are three types of secondary schools. Most pupils attend general secondary schools, where they add computer studies and more science subjects to their timetables. Particularly gifted pupils are selected for special secondary schools, where they receive extra tuition in such topics as art, music, languages or electronics. Vocational secondary schools concentrate on subjects, such as mathematics, chemistry or physics.

Higher education is important in Russia and, in 1991, around 27 out of every 10,000 people were university graduates. Students in higher education are given a small allowance from the government. In the early 1990s, about five million students were attending Russia's 519 higher educational establishments and 2,600 technical colleges.

Since the collapse of Communism, new curricula have been introduced. Textbooks and teachers now place less emphasis on political ideology. They have adopted a new approach to Russian and Soviet history and previously banned literary works are now studied.

Above: Students attending a lecture at the M. V. Lomonosov State University in Moscow. The university was founded in 1755, and today has about 20,000 full-time students.

Below: The exterior of the M. V. Lomonosov State University in Moscow. It is generally regarded as the most prestigious of Russia's institutions of higher education.

The arts

Outside the country, the art of European Russia is best known, but the country has many cultures. In the northwest, the Sami (Lapps) carry on traditional handicrafts in bone and leather. In eastern Siberia, strong Mongol, Chinese and even Japanese influences are apparent in painting, literature and music.

The best known Russian paintings are icons, religious pictures painted on wooden panels by artists of the Eastern Orthodox Church. In the early 20th century, Russian artists developed modern styles. But both eventually settled outside Russia. Under the Soviet government, artists were encouraged to use a straight-forward style, called 'socialist realism', but today there is complete freedom for artists.

Russia is also known for its performing arts, especially ballet. The Maryinsky (formerly Kirov) Ballet of St Petersburg and the Bolshoi Ballet of Moscow are world-famous.

Above: A religious icon painting from the Solovetsky Cloister.

Left: A dancer with Moscow's Bolshoi Theatre Ballet makes a spectacular leap. The world of ballet was dominated by Russia during the late 1800s and early 1900s.

Russian music is particularly noted for the operas of such composers as Modest Mussorgsky (1839-1881) and Nikolai Rimsky-Korsakov (1844-1908), and the ballet music of Peter Ilich Tchaikovsky (1840-1893) and Igor Stravinsky (1882-1971). Stravinsky, who like many other musicians left the Soviet Union, was one of the most influential of the 20th century composers. Sergei Prokofiev (1819-1953) and Dmitri Shostakovich (1906-1975) remained there.

Anton Chekhov (1860-1904) is regarded as the greatest Russian dramatist. His plays have been translated into every major language. Fyodor Dostoyevsky (1821-1881) and Leo Tolstoy (1828-1910) were major novelists. Modern writers include Boris Pasternak (1890-1960) and Mikhail Sholokov (1905-1984). Alexander Solzhenitsyn (1918-), who won the Nobel Prize for Literature in 1970, was exiled from Russia from 1974 to 1994.

Russian film-makers included the director Sergei Eisenstein (1898-1948), whose 'Potemkin' (1925) is a cinematic classic.

Above left: A member of the State Chorus of Kuban Cossacks.

Above right: A scene from 'Ivan the Terrible', a film made in the 1940s by Sergei Eisenstein.

Below: Yevgeny Yevtushenko is a poet whose works commented on Soviet society.

The making of modern Russia

The Romanov family ruled Russia for more than 300 years. When the Czar, Nicholas II, was forced to abdicate in 1917, his country had hardly developed from a medieval, feudal state. The czars ruled as dictators. Most of the people were treated little better than slaves.

In 1914 Russia joined World War I against Germany and Austria. Nicholas took personal command of his armies, leaving the Czarina Alexandra to rule. She was under the influence of a dissolute priest, Grigori Rasputin. Russia fell into chaos. Its armies lost battles, and food and fuel were scarce. Workers rioted and went on strike.

In March 1917 soldiers in the capital Petrograd (now St. Petersburg) mutinied. The czar was forced to abdicate, and a temporary government was set up. An exiled communist, Vladimir Lenin (1870–1924), returned to Russia and seized power in a second revolution, helped by a group of Communists known as Bolsheviks. They made peace with Germany in 1918. In 1922, they proclaimed the new Union of Soviet Socialist Republics (USSR), which included Russia.

Above: The last Czar, Nicholas II, who came to the throne in 1894, with the Czarina Alexandra.

Below left: A crowd of Bolsheviks demonstrate.

Below: Vladimir Lenin led the Bolsheviks in the Russian Revolution of November 1917.

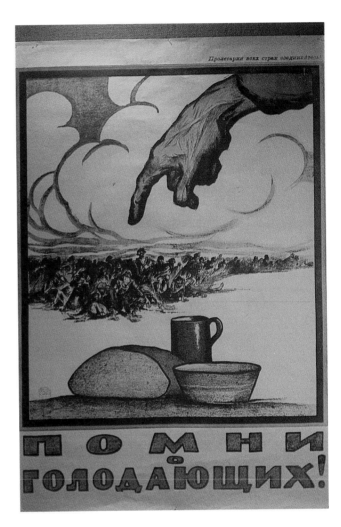

After the revolutions of 1917 the country was torn by civil war between the Red Army of the Bolsheviks, led by Lenin's second-in-command, Leon Trotsky, and the White Army of the anti-Communists. Lenin's Red Army won but Lenin himself died shortly after the new Soviet Union was proclaimed. The Communist secretary-general, Joseph Stalin (1879-1953), seized power.

Stalin introduced a brutal programme of industrialization. Kulaks, wealthy peasant farmers, had their lands confiscated, and all farming was organized into collectives. Stalin's secret police removed all his political enemies. It is estimated that 20,000,000 people were murdered, tortured or imprisoned without trial.

In 1941, during World War II, the Germans invaded the Soviet Union. Stalin and the Soviet armed forces played a major part in defeating Germany in 1945.

Above: Posters were often used to convey political messages. One (left) is a Bolshevik campaign poster; the other (right) remembers the starving.

Below: In 1945, just before the end of World War II, Stalin (right) met with Roosevelt of the United States and Churchill (left) of Britain to agree the post-war structure of eastern Europe.

Russia in the modern world

After 1945, the Soviet Union, suspicious of
Western hostility towards Communism,
determined that it would never again be
invaded. An 'arms race' developed between
the Soviet Union, a world superpower, and its
allies in eastern Europe, and Western Europe,
supported by the USA, the other superpower.

A long period of hostility called the 'cold
war' began. But by the early 1980s, the high
cost of financing the country's defences
crippled the Soviet economy. In 1985, Mikhail
Gorbachev (1931-) became the Soviet leader.
He introduced new policies, including a new
openness in government, called glasnost,
economic reforms called perestroika
(restructuring) and increased freedom of
speech. The 'cold war' came to an end and
relations with the West improved.

Gorbachev's reforms led to debates about
the future of the Soviet Union. He wanted to
keep the 15 republics of the Soviet Union
united. But, in 1990 the governments of the
republics declared that their laws took
precedence over Soviet laws.

Above: The face of
Russian cosmonaut Yuri
Gagarin, in 1961 the first
man to travel in space,
dominates the Moscow
Cosmos Space Pavilion.

Below: Mikhail Gorbachev,
(far left), whose reforms
led to debates about the
future of the Soviet Union,
receiving the Nobel Peace
Prize in Oslo, 1990.

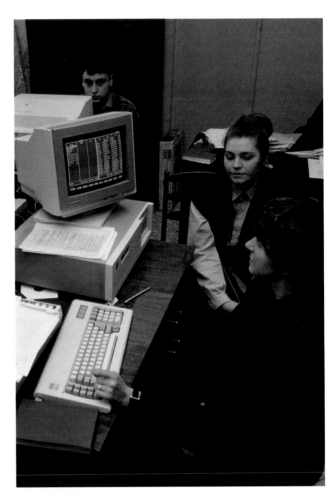

In August 1991, Communists tried to overthrow Gorbachev's government. But they were defeated by forces led by the Russian president, Boris Yeltsin (1931-). Gorbachev remained Soviet president until December 25 1991, when the Soviet Union was dissolved. Russia and the other 14 republics then became separate nations. Ties were maintained through a loose confederation called the Commonwealth of Independent Nations (CIS) which, by 1994, contained all the former Soviet republics except for Estonia, Latvia and Lithuania.

In Russia, Yeltsin, supported by Western governments, pushed ahead with reforms, though he had to put down another rebellion in October 1993. A new constitution was adopted in 1993 and multiparty, parliamentary elections were held. Although the reforms have caused great upheaval, most experts believe that Russia, with its huge resources and skilled work force, will overcome its current problems.

Above left: Crowds watch a tank near Parliament during the rebellion in October 1993.

Above right: A commercial bank. Experts believe that Russia's resources and skilled work force will see it through its problems.

Below: American President Bill Clinton meets Boris Yeltsin in Moscow in January 1994.

Fact file: government and world role

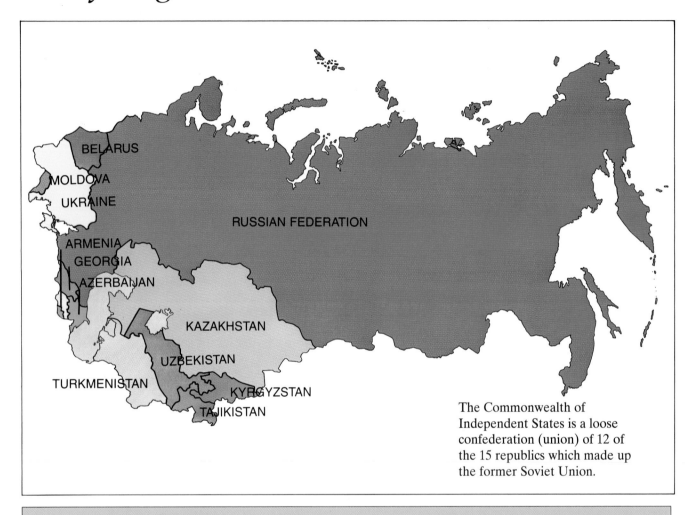

BELARUS
MOLDOVA
UKRAINE
ARMENIA
GEORGIA
AZERBAIJAN
RUSSIAN FEDERATION
KAZAKHSTAN
UZBEKISTAN
TURKMENISTAN
KYRGYZSTAN
TAJIKISTAN

The Commonwealth of Independent States is a loose confederation (union) of 12 of the 15 republics which made up the former Soviet Union.

Key Facts

Official name: Rossiyskaya Federatsiya (Russian Federation) or Rossiya (Russia).
Flag: Tricolour: three horizontal stripes of white (top), blue (centre) and red (bottom).
National anthem: No words; tune from an opera by the Russian composer Mikhail Glinka.
National government: Russia is a multiparty federal republic. The head of state is the directly elected President, who may not be elected to more than two four-year terms. The President is responsible for foreign policy and is Commander-in Chief of the Armed Forces. The President may, under certain conditions, introduce martial law or a state of emergency. The Federal Assembly (parliament) contains two houses. The upper house, the Federation Council, has 178 members, two from each of the republics, territories, provinces, autonomous areas and cities of federal status, which together make up the Federation. The lower house, the State Duma, has 450 deputies elected to four-year terms. The government is made up of a Chairman, nominated by the President and approved by the State Duma, a Vice-Chairman and federal ministers.

Judiciary: Judges to the three highest courts are elected by the Federation Council, on presentation by the President. The Constitutional Court deals with constitutional matters, the Supreme Court with civil, criminal, administrative and other matters, and the Supreme Arbitration Court, with economic and other disputes.

Local government: Local government is carried on by the 89 members of the Russian Federation through elected and other bodies.
Armed forces: A Russian army was created in 1992. By 1994, its strength was about 1,000,000, 450,000 of whom were conscripts. Navy: Russia inherited most of the Soviet fleet, but personnel and activities were greatly reduced in the early 1990s because of lack of funds; personnel in 1993—300,000, 180,000 of whom were conscripts. Air Force: Russia has an Air Force and Air Defence Forces; combined personnel in 1993 totalled 400,000, 185,000 of whom were conscripts.
Alliances: Russia is a member of the United Nations, the UN Security Council, and the Council of Europe. In 1994, Russia signed the Partnership for Peace with NATO.

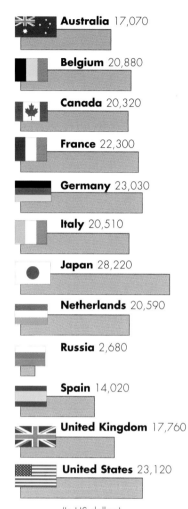

Australia	17,070	
Belgium	20,880	
Canada	20,320	
France	22,300	
Germany	23,030	
Italy	20,510	
Japan	28,220	
Netherlands	20,590	
Russia	2,680	
Spain	14,020	
United Kingdom	17,760	
United States	23,120	

(In US dollars)

△ **The Russian parliament**
Under Russia's constitution of 1993, the President, who is elected by direct suffrage for a term of four years, has sweeping powers.

▷ **National wealth created per person in 1992**
In 1992, Russia's economy was in a state of turmoil as state-run businesses were privatized and inefficient industries went out of business. This turmoil is reflected in Russia's low income per capita by comparison with Western countries.

△ **The Russian Federation**
Each of the 89 parts of Russia send two representatives to the Federation Council, the upper house in Russia's parliament.

Index